```
    c1:=2 to max_te
  if (terep_tipusok
    begin
      inc(l_tipusok
      l_tipusok[l_t
      l_tipusok[l_t
      if l_tipusok[
        l_tipusok[l_

    end;
    l_tipusok_szama=
    egin
      hiba:=30;
      kileprutin;

      tipusok_szama
      =l_tipusok[1]
      :cardinal); a
```

*Computer
programming code*

CONTENTS

INTRODUCTION

For as long as there has been written information, there have been codes.

Throughout history, codes have kept information secret:

- In ancient times, leaders sent coded orders to their armies.
- Secret government papers were written in code to protect them.
- Spies sent coded messages about their enemies.

CODE
BREAKERS

Ben Hubbard

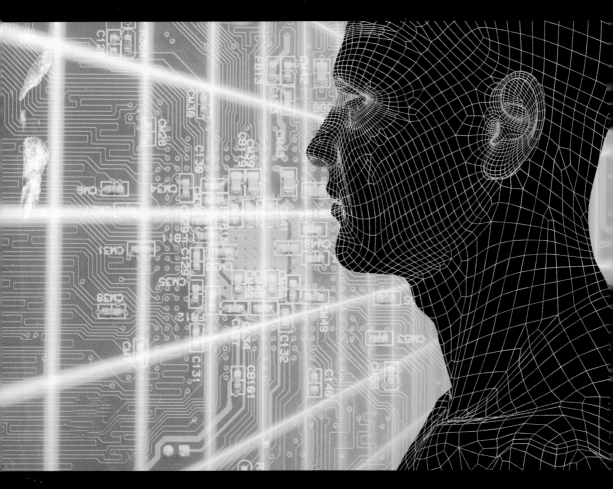

CLASH

by **Tick** **Tock** **Books**

Publisher: Melissa Fairley
Art Director: Faith Booker
Editor: Victoria Garrard
Designer: Emma Randall
Production Controller: Ed Green
Production Manager: Suzy Kelly

ISBN: 978 1 84898 215 4

Printed in China
1 3 5 7 9 10 8 6 4 2

Picture credits (t=top; b=bottom; c=centre; l=left; r=right; OFC=outside front cover; OBC=outside back cover):
A. Barrington Brown/Science Photo Library: 7tr. AFP/Getty Images: 24. Bettmann/Corbis: 14, 15. iStock: OFCl, OFCr, 1,
25, 27. Mehau Kulyk/Science Photo Library: 28–29. Stephen Mulcahey/Alamy: 12–13. Science and Society/SuperStock:
8–9. Science Source/Science Photo Library: 7tl, 7tc. Shutterstock: OFC (background), 2, 4 (both), 5, 6–7, 10, 11 (both),
16t, 20–21, 22, 23, 26, OBC (background). SSPL via Getty Images: 16b, 19. Volker Steger/Science Photo Library: 29.
Time & Life Pictures/Getty Images: 17, 18.

Thank you to Lorraine Petersen and the members of nasen

Every effort has been made to trace copyright holders, and we apologize in advance for any omissions.
We would be pleased to insert the appropriate acknowledgements in any subsequent edition of this publication.

NOTE TO READERS
The website addresses are correct at the time of publishing. However, due to the ever-changing
nature of the Internet, websites and content may change. Some websites can contain links
that are unsuitable for children. The publisher is not responsible for changes in content or
website addresses. We advise that Internet searches are be supervised by an adult.

But as long as there have been codes,
there have been people to break them.

When computers were invented machines
partly replaced humans as code breakers.

NATURE'S CODE

Most codes have been created by humans or machines. But the most complicated code was created by nature: DNA.

DNA is a molecule that carries the genetic code of a living thing. Your DNA is responsible for what colour of eyes you have and how tall you are. It is your DNA that makes you unique!

A double helix

Nobody knew much about this genetic code until the 1950s, when scientists Rosalind Franklin, James Watson and Francis Crick made the breakthrough. They discovered DNA looked like two spirals, called a double helix.

James Watson

Rosalind Franklin

Francis Crick

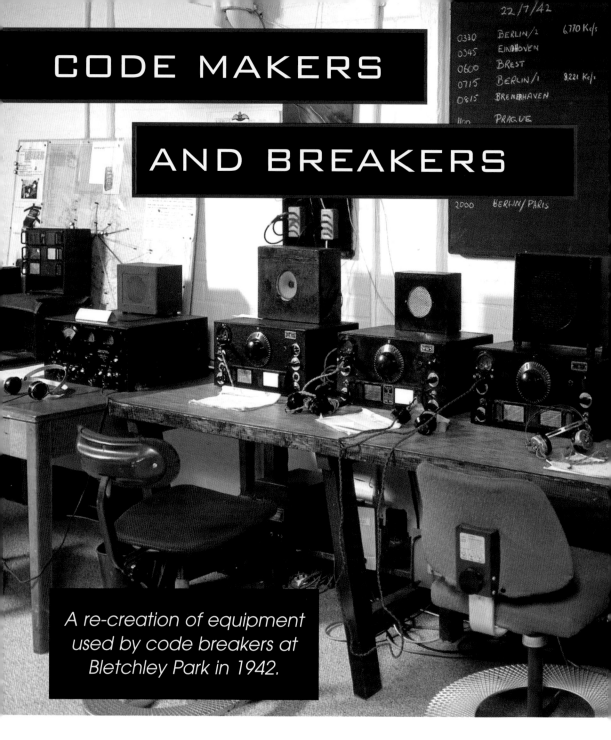

CODE MAKERS
AND BREAKERS

A re-creation of equipment used by code breakers at Bletchley Park in 1942.

A person who turns writing into a secret code is called a cryptographer.

Creating a code is called encryption.

A person who breaks a cryptographer's code is called a cryptanalyst.

Throughout history, cryptographers have thought their codes were unbreakable. But cryptanalysts have always proved them wrong.

THE LOST CODE

We know codes have been around for as long as human history. So what if there were codes that had been lost in the mists of time?

Some believe a forgotten code was used by people across the world thousands of years ago. They say ancient civilizations used this code to build temples, palaces and tombs in precise locations on different continents.

Stonehenge, England

Some people think the code was part of an early Global Positioning System (GPS). They believe the location of Stonehenge links directly to the Great Pyramid in Egypt. They say modern GPS is helping to prove the code is real.

Others say the code is just a coincidence.

The Great Pyramid, Egypt

THE CAESAR SHIFT

The Roman leader Julius Caesar invented a very easy letter code.

Caesar wrote a message and then replaced each letter with the letter in the alphabet three places along. For example, "A" would be written as "D" and "B" as "E".

Sometimes the code would change to four places along in the alphabet, or five.

NAVAJO TALKERS

During World War II, the United States needed a new code to protect messages against the Japanese, their enemy.

Navajo warriors

Navajo signalmen

The Japanese never broke the code.

ENIGMA

By World War II the Germans had created the greatest code-making machine ever invented.

The machine was called Enigma and the odds of breaking its code were 150 million million to one.

In 1939, the Polish scientist Marian Rejewski built a replica Enigma to try and crack it. When war broke out he sent everything he knew to the code breakers based at Bletchley Park, England.

In 1940, Alan Turing (see pages 18–19), cracked Enigma. From that point on Britain could unscramble Germany's many codes.

German soldiers sending a message using the Enigma machine.

ALAN TURING

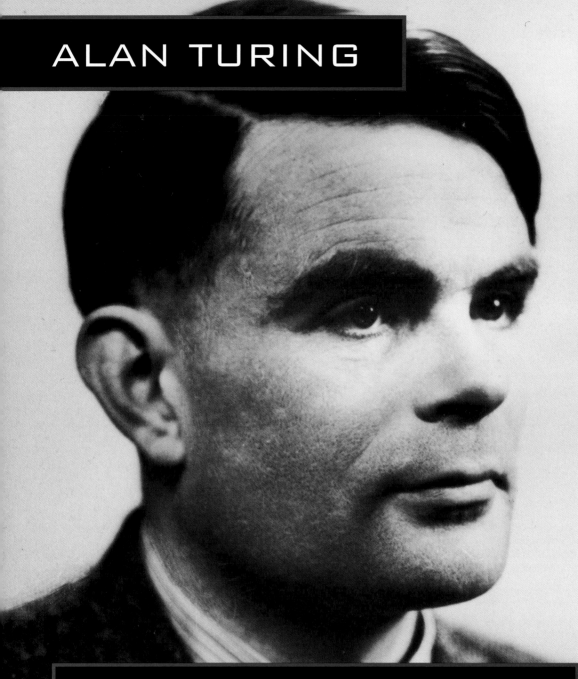

Name: Alan Turing
Profile: An English mathematician, code breaker and one of the founders of modern computer science.
Code broken: Enigma
Year: 1940

capable of solving all mathematical problems.

The pilot ACE
computer

**"We can only see a short distance ahead, but
we can see plenty there that needs to be done."
– Alan Turing**

COMPUTER CODES

The Enigma machine changed cryptography forever. Now for the first time, computers could create codes as well as humans.

The most common modern computer code is called "public key encryption". This uses a public key and a private key. The public key is used to encrypt text, such as an email. The private key is then used to read this encoded text.

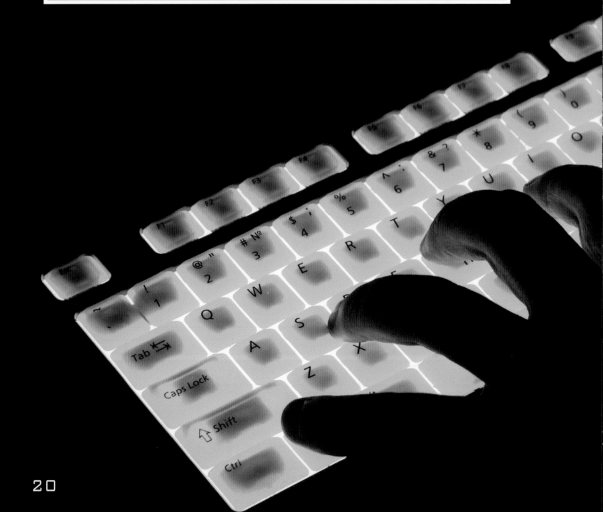

Lots of people can use the public key to encrypt information. However, only the person with the private key will be able to read the information. This allows people to send private information to each other securely.

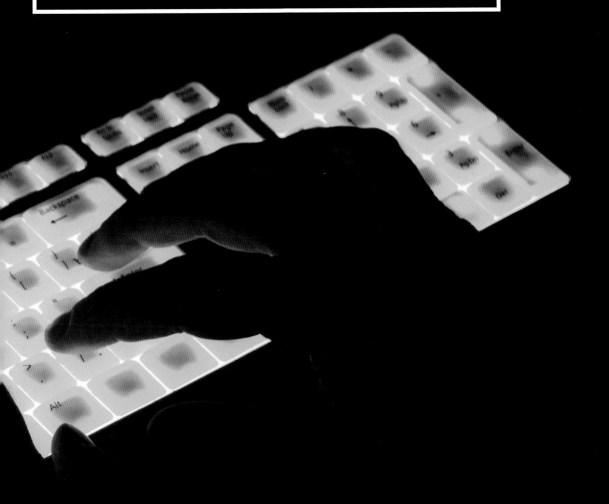

COMPUTER HACKERS

Today, computers constantly encrypt information.

This stops people stealing our credit card details or reading our emails.

But if there is a code to break, there will always be code breakers itching to crack it.

The modern cryptanalyst is the computer hacker. Hackers illegally break into top secret computer systems.

Computer programming code

They do this to steal, to prove computer systems are not secure – **or just for the challenge!**

GARY MCKINNON

"It was like a real game. It was addictive. Hugely addictive."
- Gary McKinnon

Name: Gary McKinnon

Profile: Scotsman who has been called "the biggest military computer hacker of all time".

Codes broken: Gary hacked into US government agency computers belonging to the National Aeronautics and Space Administration (NASA), the US Army, Navy and Air Force and the Department of Defense.

Year: 2001–2002

Other information: Gary said he was hacking to look for evidence of unidentified flying objects (UFOs).

CAPTCHA

Hackers live to crack computer codes, but can a computer crack a human code?

You've probably seen a CAPTCHA code. It often pops up on a website as a line of wavy letters, which you have to type in.

The code makes sure the user is human. It stops computers automatically sending spam and viruses to other computers.

But hackers are teaching computers to break CAPTCHA codes. Experts think this will lead to artificial intelligence (AI) – the ability for computers to think for themselves.

QUANTUM COMPUTERS

Making and breaking codes has always relied on mathematics – calculated either by humans or computers.

But soon quantum computers will make the codes for us. They are the super computers of the future. These computers are based on physics, not mathematics.

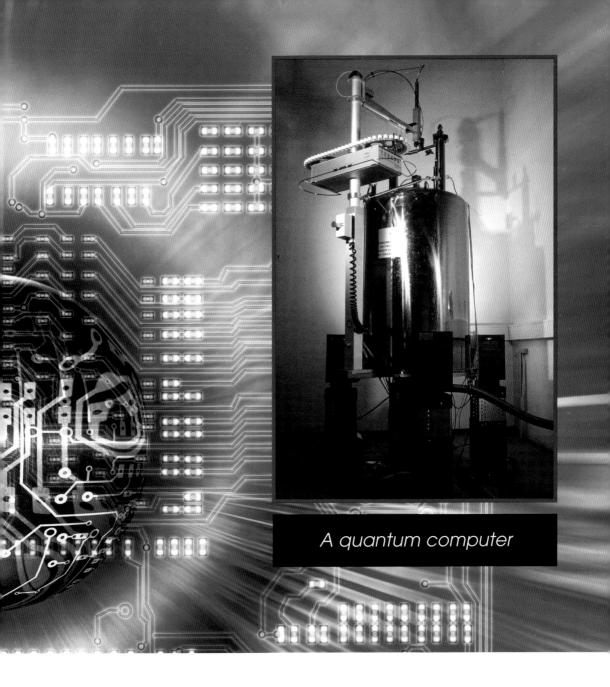

A quantum computer

However, scientists do know that quantum computers will be able to make unbreakable codes, and also break any code ever created.

NEED TO KNOW WORDS

battleship A heavy warship.

coincidence Things happening at the same time or place by chance.

DNA Deoxyribonucleic acid. A type of acid that carries the genetic information in a cell.

encrypt To put into a code so that unauthorized people can't read it.

Global Positioning System (GPS) A navigational system that uses satellites to give exact locations.

hacker Someone who uses programming skills to gain illegal access to a computer.

helix A spiral shape or structure.

mathematician An expert in mathematics.

Navajo A Native American people.

physics A type of science that deals with matter and energy.

spy A special agent employed by a country to find out secret information.

DID YOU KNOW?

Nobody could read Egyptian hieroglyphs until 1799, after the famous Rosetta stone was found. Frenchman Jean-François Champollion managed to translate the language from the writing inscribed on the tablet.

FIND OUT MORE ONLINE

The Central Intelligence Agency (CIA) website dedicated to breaking codes, with games and puzzles plus information about the everyday work of the CIA:
https://www.cia.gov/kids-page/index.html

National Security Agency (NSA) CryptKids site, provides an introduction to codes plus quizzes for future code makers and code breakers:
http://www.nsa.gov/kids

Planet Science is full of fun activities and quizzes:
http://www.scienceyear.com/outthere/index.html?page=/outthere/spy/index.html

INDEX